Microeconomics Made Easy For Beginners

Roggie Clark

Avoid Credit Card Debt With This Book

Are you tired of living paycheck to paycheck? Drowning in interest rates and minimum payments that never seem to shrink your balance? *Understanding & Overcoming Credit Card Debt* is your roadmap to financial freedom.

https://www.amazon.com/dp/B0F3WCVWG8

Avoid Wasting Money On Crypto With This Book

Whether you're curious, cautious, or ready to invest, this book breaks down complex topics into plain language and cuts through the noise, buzzwords, and get-rich-quick schemes.

https://www.amazon.com/Think-Before-You-Crypto-Understanding-ebook/dp/B0F3YQ1L2Q

Learn How To Invest in Gold Bars With This Book

Whether you're new to investing or seeking to diversify your portfolio, this beginner-friendly guide will give you the knowledge and confidence to invest in gold, and other precious metals.

https://www.amazon.com/Ultimate-Investing-Buying-Guide-Beginners-ebook/dp/B0F1KWWDXG

Learn How To Invest in Silver With This Book

Whether you're approaching retirement or already enjoying it, protecting and growing your wealth is critical. The Ultimate Silver Investing & Buying Guide For Beginners is your clear, no-nonsense guide to incorporating silver into your wealth-building strategy.

https://www.amazon.com/Ultimate-Silver-Investing-Buying-Beginners-ebook

Copyright

Title: Microeconomics Made Easy For Beginners
Author: Roggie Clark

Disclaimer

The views and opinions expressed in this book are those of the author and do not necessarily reflect the official policy or position of any individual, company, or organization cited or referenced in the text. The author is not affiliated with any of the individuals, companies, or organizations mentioned in the text, nor does the author receive any form of compensation for citing or referencing them.

The professional information in this text is distributed on an "as is" basis, without warranty. While every precaution has been taken in the preparation of the text, neither the author nor the publisher shall have any liability to any person or entity with respect to any loss or damage caused or alleged to be caused directly or indirectly by the instructions contained in this text or by the computer software and hardware products described in it.

The author nor the publisher does not guarantee any specific results or outcomes, and the information provided in this text should not be construed as professional advice. Readers should always consult with a qualified professional before making any significant changes to their website or business.

By reading this text, you agree that the author nor the publisher is responsible for any direct, indirect, incidental, or consequential damages that may arise from the use of the information provided. You assume full responsibility for any actions taken based on the information presented in this text.

College Or University Usage

I recommend that college deans and professors consider this book for their curriculum; as well as a resource for your students to use for their own research. If you are interested in using the book for your course or having your bookstore source it for students to purchase, you can reach out to me directly.

Please email me at **bouncerankseo@gmail.com**. In your email, please include the following information:

- Your name
- The school you represent
- The class size you are teaching
- The length of your course (e.g. 6-week course, 12-week course, etc.)
- Any other important information I should know

My administrative assistant will email you back within 24 - 48 hours with rates, and an information sheet to use for your class.

Table of Contents

Introduction

Microeconomics is often introduced as the study of supply and demand, prices, and consumer behavior. While that is technically correct, it barely scratches the surface of what microeconomics truly represents.

At its core, microeconomics is the study of incentives and decision making under constraint.

It examines how individuals, households, and firms allocate limited resources. It explores why consumers buy certain products, why businesses set prices the way they do, why some industries become competitive while others concentrate power, and how small choices ripple outward into larger market outcomes.

If macroeconomics studies the economy from a high altitude, microeconomics zooms in to street level. It focuses on the choices of buyers and sellers, the structure of individual markets, and the strategic behavior of firms operating under competition and uncertainty.

Understanding microeconomics matters whether you are:

- A student trying to grasp economic theory

- A business owner making pricing decisions
- A marketer analyzing consumer behavior
- Or simply someone trying to understand why markets behave the way they do

Markets do not move randomly. They move because individuals respond to incentives. Every price change, every product launch, every advertising campaign, every regulatory rule, all of it alters incentives. And when incentives change, behavior changes.

This book will help you understand:

- How supply and demand interact to determine prices
- Why elasticity shapes revenue and pricing strategy
- How consumers make choices under budget constraints
- How firms manage production and costs
- Why different market structures produce different outcomes
- How strategic behavior and game theory influence competition
- Where markets succeed and where they fail

But this is not a book of abstract graphs and memorized formulas.

It is a framework for thinking.

Throughout these chapters, you will see that economic models are useful, but they are not perfect. Consumers are not always rational. Firms do not operate in frictionless environments. Information is incomplete. Regulations distort incentives. Emotions shape demand. Barriers to entry protect incumbents.

Microeconomics is powerful precisely because it forces us to examine trade offs. There is no decision without cost. There is no pricing strategy without consequence. There is no policy without unintended effects.

The goal is not to memorize curves.

The goal is to understand behavior.

Once you understand incentives, constraints, and strategic interaction, you will begin to see markets differently. You will recognize patterns in pricing, production, competition, and regulation. You will understand why some businesses thrive while others collapse. You will see why certain policies generate distortions. And most importantly, you will be able to think critically rather than react emotionally.

Microeconomics is not just about small units of analysis.

It is about the small decisions that collectively shape entire systems.

Let's begin.

Chapter 1: Supply, Demand, and the Logic of Market Prices

Markets do not set prices randomly.

Prices emerge from millions of individual decisions made by buyers and sellers responding to incentives. When those incentives shift, prices shift. When prices shift, behavior shifts.

Supply and demand is not just an introductory concept. It is the foundational logic behind how decentralized systems coordinate activity without central direction.

To understand microeconomics, you must understand this mechanism deeply, not just graphically.

The Law of Demand

Demand reflects how much of a good or service consumers are willing and able to purchase at various price levels.

The law of demand states that, all else equal, as price rises, quantity demanded falls. As price falls, quantity demanded rises.

This relationship exists because of two core forces:

1. Substitution effect
   When prices rise, consumers look for alternatives.
2. Income effect
   Higher prices reduce purchasing power, limiting consumption.

But demand is not driven by price alone.

It is shaped by:

- Consumer income
- Preferences
- Expectations
- Prices of substitutes
- Prices of complementary goods
- Cultural and psychological influences

Demand curves slope downward because people face trade offs. Every dollar spent on one product cannot be spent elsewhere.

The Law of Supply

Supply reflects how much of a good or service producers are willing and able to offer at various price levels.

The law of supply states that, all else equal, as price rises, quantity supplied rises. As price falls, quantity supplied falls.

Higher prices increase profitability. Increased profitability attracts more production.

But supply is also influenced by:

- Input costs
- Technology
- Government regulation
- Taxes and subsidies
- Expectations of future prices
- Access to capital

Supply curves slope upward because firms respond to profit incentives.

The Supply Curve and Demand Curve

Economists use ***curves*** to visualize how supply and demand respond to price changes. These curves provide a snapshot of economic behavior in a given market. Below is an example of a **Supply** and **Demand Curve**:

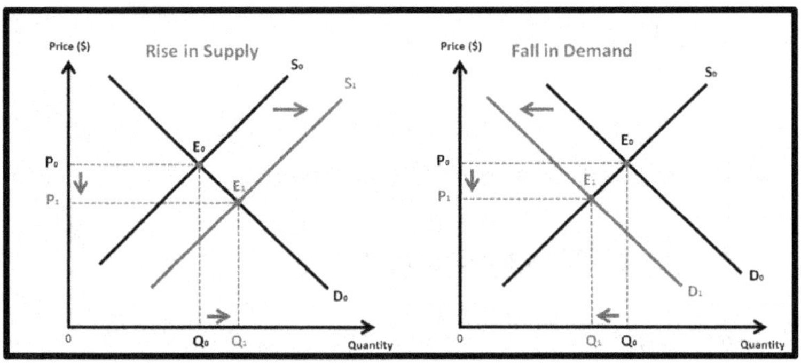

Caption: Supply and demand curves visually illustrate how a product's price relates to the quantities that producers are willing to sell and consumers are willing to buy. The supply and demand curves illustrate market equilibrium (Ansari, 2023, Figure 1).

Market Equilibrium

Market equilibrium occurs where quantity demanded equals quantity supplied.

At this price:

- There is no shortage
- There is no surplus
- The market clears

Equilibrium is not a moral outcome. It is not necessarily fair. It is not necessarily optimal. It is simply the price at which voluntary exchange balances.

If price is set above equilibrium:

- Supply exceeds demand.
- A surplus emerges.

If price is set below equilibrium:

- Demand exceeds supply.
- A shortage emerges.

Prices act as signals. Shortages signal producers to increase output. Surpluses signal producers to reduce output.

This signaling function is what allows markets to coordinate activity without central planning.

Below, is example of a graph showing Market Equilibrium in action:

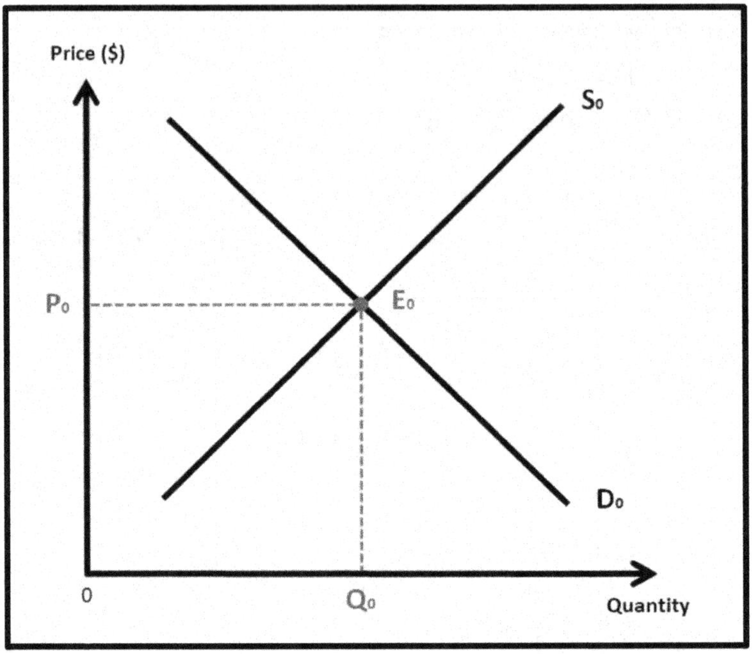

Graph that illustrates market equilibrium (Ansari, 2023, Figure 2).

When Equilibrium Is Disrupted

Markets rarely remain static.

External shocks can shift supply or demand:

- Rising incomes increase demand.
- New technology increases supply.
- Input cost spikes reduce supply.
- Cultural trends reshape preferences.

- Geopolitical disruptions affect trade.

When either curve shifts, equilibrium changes.

The result is new price signals, new production decisions, and new consumer behavior.

Understanding these shifts allows business owners and policymakers to anticipate rather than react.

Price Controls and Market Distortions

Sometimes governments intervene. Price ceilings attempt to keep prices below equilibrium. Price floors attempt to keep prices above equilibrium.

While often well intentioned, these interventions distort signals.

A price ceiling below equilibrium creates persistent shortages. Black markets may emerge. Quality may decline.

A price floor above equilibrium creates surpluses. Excess supply may require subsidies or storage.

The key lesson is not ideological.

It is structural.

When prices cannot adjust freely, other mechanisms adjust instead, often inefficiently.

Deadweight Loss and Efficiency

When markets operate at equilibrium under competitive conditions, total surplus is maximized.

Total surplus includes:

- Consumer surplus
- Producer surplus

Interventions such as taxes, subsidies, or binding price controls create deadweight loss, meaning some mutually beneficial trades no longer occur.

Deadweight loss represents lost efficiency.

It is not just a triangle on a graph. It represents real exchanges that never happen.

Behavioral Complications

Traditional supply and demand assumes rational actors. Reality is more complicated.

Consumers are influenced by:

- Fear of missing out
- Branding
- Social proof
- Perceived scarcity
- Status signaling

Firms may misjudge demand. Consumers may overreact to price changes. Information may be incomplete.

Markets are powerful, but they are not frictionless.

Why This Matters for Business and Strategy

For entrepreneurs and marketers, supply and demand is not theoretical.

It determines:

- Pricing power
- Inventory management
- Expansion timing
- Promotional strategy
- Market entry decisions

If demand is rising faster than supply, prices can increase.

If supply floods the market, margins shrink.

Understanding equilibrium allows businesses to anticipate pressure before it materializes.

Last Thoughts

Supply and demand is often presented as a simple graph. In reality, it is a dynamic process of constant adjustment.

Markets coordinate behavior through incentives and signals. When those signals are clear, resources flow efficiently. When they are distorted, inefficiencies emerge.

The goal is not to worship markets. The goal is not to reject them. The goal is to understand them.

When you understand supply and demand deeply, you begin to see that prices are not arbitrary numbers. They are compressed information about scarcity, preference, cost, and expectation.

And once you understand that, you can make better decisions within the system, whether as a student, policymaker, business owner, or consumer.

Chapter 2: Elasticity, Pricing Power, and Consumer Response

Not all price changes are created equal.

Sometimes a small increase in price causes sales to collapse. Other times, prices rise significantly and demand barely moves. The difference between those two outcomes is elasticity.

Elasticity is not just a mathematical concept. It is a measure of power.

It tells us who has flexibility, who has leverage, and where vulnerability exists in a market.

If supply and demand explain how prices are formed, elasticity explains how sensitive behavior is once those prices move.

What Is Price Elasticity of Demand

Price Elasticity of Demand measures how responsive quantity demanded is to a change in price.

If a small price increase causes a large drop in quantity demanded, demand is elastic.

If a price increase causes only a small change in quantity demanded, demand is inelastic.

Formally, elasticity is calculated as:

Percentage change in quantity demanded divided by percentage change in price.

But the formula is only useful if you understand what it represents.

Elasticity measures behavioral sensitivity.

What Determines Elasticity

Elasticity is shaped by structural and psychological forces:

1. Availability of substitutes
   The more alternatives consumers have, the more elastic demand becomes.
2. Necessity versus luxury
   Essential goods tend to be more inelastic.
   Discretionary goods are typically more elastic.

3. Proportion of income
   Goods that consume a large portion of income tend to be more elastic.
4. Time horizon
   Demand is usually more elastic in the long run than in the short run because consumers adjust behavior over time.
5. Brand loyalty and perceived differentiation
   Strong brands can reduce elasticity by limiting substitution.

Elasticity is not fixed. It changes with context.

Gasoline may appear inelastic in the short run, but over time consumers shift to electric vehicles, public transportation, or relocation. What was once inelastic becomes elastic.

Elasticity and Revenue

Elasticity directly affects total revenue.

If demand is elastic:

- Lowering price increases total revenue.
- Raising price decreases total revenue.

If demand is inelastic:

- Raising price increases total revenue.
- Lowering price decreases total revenue.

This is where elasticity becomes strategic.Businesses with inelastic demand have pricing power. Businesses facing elastic demand compete aggressively on price.

Understanding elasticity prevents destructive pricing mistakes.

Cross Elasticity of Demand

Markets are interconnected.

Cross Elasticity measures how demand for one good changes when the price of another good changes.

If two goods are substitutes, an increase in the price of one increases demand for the other.

If two goods are complements, an increase in the price of one decreases demand for the other.

This is not just theory.

It determines:

- Competitive strategy
- Bundling decisions
- Market positioning
- Partnership opportunities

A coffee company must understand how the price of sugar affects its demand.A streaming platform must understand how competitor pricing influences subscriptions.

Cross elasticity reveals competitive interdependence.

Income Elasticity of Demand

Income Elasticity measures how demand changes when consumer income changes.

Normal goods experience increased demand as income rises. Inferior goods may see demand decline as income rises.

Luxury goods tend to have high income elasticity. Staple goods tend to have low income elasticity.

This matters for long term positioning.

Companies that depend heavily on income sensitive demand are vulnerable to recessions.

Elasticity and Strategic Pricing

Elasticity is a lens for decision making.

Consider the following:

- A company with strong brand loyalty can raise prices gradually with minimal loss of demand.
- A commodity producer must compete aggressively because substitutes are abundant.
- A firm entering a competitive market may intentionally price low to increase elasticity temporarily and capture share.
- A monopolist may price strategically to avoid regulatory backlash while preserving long term profit.

Elasticity shapes not only pricing, but also marketing investment, product differentiation, and expansion strategy.

Behavioral Elasticity

Traditional models assume rational response. Reality is more nuanced.

Consumers may tolerate price increases if:

- The increase is gradual.
- The increase is framed as necessary.
- The brand is emotionally trusted.
- The product signals status.

Conversely, sudden price shocks may trigger overreaction. Perception influences elasticity.

A five percent increase may feel different depending on context, communication, and expectation.

Elasticity is partly psychological.

Limits of Elasticity Analysis

Elasticity is powerful, but incomplete.

It assumes:

- Accurate measurement of demand response.
- Stable consumer preferences.
- Predictable substitution patterns.

In reality:

- Data may be noisy.
- Competitors may react strategically.
- Supply constraints may distort outcomes.
- Regulations may cap pricing flexibility.

Elasticity informs decisions, but it does not guarantee outcomes.

Why Elasticity Matters Beyond Business

Elasticity also shapes public policy.

Taxes on inelastic goods generate higher revenue with smaller reductions in consumption.

Taxes on elastic goods distort behavior more dramatically.

Minimum wage laws, healthcare pricing, energy subsidies, and rent control all involve implicit elasticity assumptions.

When policymakers misjudge elasticity, unintended consequences follow.

Last Thoughts

Elasticity is about responsiveness. It reveals where flexibility exists and where constraints bind tightly.

It shows who absorbs cost increases and who passes them forward. It reveals which firms have power and which must compete aggressively.

More importantly, elasticity forces us to confront trade offs. There is no pricing decision without consequence. There is no revenue strategy without risk. There is no competitive move without response.

Understanding elasticity means understanding reaction.

And in markets, reaction determines outcome.

Chapter 3: Utility, Choice, and the Architecture of Decision Making

Demand curves do not move on their own. They move because individuals make choices.

Behind every purchase is a decision. Behind every decision is a comparison. Behind every comparison is an attempt, whether conscious or not, to maximize satisfaction within limits.

Microeconomics calls that satisfaction utility.

But utility is not about happiness in the abstract. It is about trade offs.

Every choice implies sacrifice. Every purchase excludes another possibility. Every allocation of time or money reflects priority.

To understand markets, we must understand how individuals choose.

What Is Utility

Utility represents the satisfaction or benefit a person derives from consuming a good or service.

It is subjective.

The same product may provide high utility to one person and little to another. A luxury handbag may represent status and identity to one consumer, and unnecessary expense to another.

Utility is not measurable in absolute terms. It cannot be observed directly. It can only be inferred through behavior.

Economists historically distinguished between two ways of thinking about utility:

Cardinal utility assumes satisfaction can be measured numerically.

Ordinal utility assumes preferences can only be ranked.

Modern microeconomics relies primarily on ordinal utility. Consumers do not assign exact numbers to satisfaction. They rank options and choose what they prefer.

This shift reflects realism.

We cannot quantify happiness precisely, but we can observe preference.

Total Utility and Marginal Utility

Understanding how satisfaction changes as consumption increases is central to predicting behavior.

Total Utility represents the overall satisfaction from consuming a certain quantity of a good.

Marginal Utility represents the additional satisfaction gained from consuming one more unit.

This distinction matters because of one of the most powerful principles in microeconomics:

The Law of Diminishing Marginal Utility

As consumption increases, the additional satisfaction gained from each extra unit tends to decline.

The first slice of pizza satisfies hunger. The second slice still provides pleasure. By the fourth slice, satisfaction decreases. Beyond that, consumption may even generate discomfort.

This principle explains why demand curves slope downward. Consumers are only willing to purchase additional units at lower prices because each additional unit provides less marginal benefit.

Diminishing marginal utility is not about boredom. It is about saturation.

Utility and Budget Constraints

Choice does not occur in a vacuum. Consumers face constraints.

Income limits consumption possibilities. Time limits consumption possibilities. Information limits evaluation.

A budget constraint represents the combinations of goods a consumer can afford given income and prices.

Consumers attempt to maximize utility within that constraint.

Optimal choice occurs where the marginal benefit per dollar spent is equal across goods.

In simpler terms:

Consumers allocate spending where it produces the greatest additional satisfaction relative to cost.

If one product delivers more satisfaction per dollar than another, spending shifts toward it.

This reallocation continues until equilibrium is reached within the individual's budget.

Indifference Curves and Trade Offs

Indifference curves represent combinations of goods that yield equal satisfaction.

They illustrate substitution.

If a consumer is willing to give up two cups of coffee for one smoothie while maintaining the same satisfaction, that trade off reflects preference structure.

The slope of the indifference curve, called the Marginal Rate of Substitution, reflects the rate at which a consumer is willing to substitute one good for another.

When the marginal rate of substitution equals the price ratio of goods, utility is maximized.

This is not about geometry. It is about alignment between subjective preference and objective cost.

Beyond Rationality: Behavioral Complications

Consumer Choice Theory assumes rationality. But humans are not perfectly rational.

Behavioral economics demonstrates that:

- People anchor to initial prices.
- They overvalue losses relative to gains.
- They exhibit present bias.
- They respond to framing effects.
- They follow social signals.
- They make impulse purchases.

Preferences are not always stable. They shift with context. They evolve with experience. They are influenced by advertising.

Utility maximization remains a useful model, but it is incomplete.

Real decision making blends logic, emotion, habit, and social influence.

Types of Utility in Applied Markets

While theoretical utility explains satisfaction, applied utility explains how value is delivered in real markets.

Businesses create value through:

- Form utility, transforming raw inputs into usable goods.
- Place utility, making products available where needed.
- Time utility, making products available when needed.
- Possession utility, enabling ownership or access.
- Information utility, communicating value clearly.
- Service utility, enhancing experience beyond the core product.

These utilities interact.

A product may have strong form utility but fail without place utility. A service may have high information utility but weak service support.

Understanding these layers allows firms to engineer satisfaction rather than hope for it.

Long Term Choice and Opportunity Cost

Utility is often framed in short term consumption.

But real decisions often involve long term trade offs.

Choosing education over immediate income. Choosing investment over consumption. Choosing brand loyalty over lower price.

Every decision involves opportunity cost, the value of the next best alternative.

Opportunity cost is invisible, but real.

It shapes consumption patterns, saving behavior, and career choices.

Utility is maximized not just across products, but across time.

Why This Matters for Strategy

For businesses and marketers, understanding consumer choice is critical.

If marginal utility declines quickly, pricing must reflect sensitivity.

If brand identity increases perceived utility, differentiation reduces elasticity.

If consumers are budget constrained, premium positioning must justify value clearly.

Firms that understand utility structure can:

- Design better pricing tiers.
- Structure bundles strategically.
- Emphasize features that enhance perceived value.
- Reduce substitution risk.
- Anticipate behavioral biases.

Utility explains why people buy. But constraints explain what they can buy.

The intersection determines outcome.

Last Thoughts

Utility and Consumer Choice Theory provide a structured way to analyze decision making.

But they are not about perfect rationality. They are about constrained optimization in imperfect conditions.

Consumers pursue satisfaction, but within limits.
They evaluate trade offs, but not always logically.
They maximize value, but through subjective perception.

Markets function because millions of these decisions aggregate.

If you understand how individuals allocate resources under constraint, you understand how demand emerges.

And when you understand demand, you understand leverage.

Microeconomics does not begin with firms. It begins with choice.

Chapter 4: Production, Costs, and the Logic of Firm Behavior

Consumers allocate income. Firms allocate capital. Every business decision, hiring, investing, expanding, discounting, shutting down, is a response to costs, expected revenue, and uncertainty.

Production is not just about making goods. It is about converting inputs into outputs efficiently under constraint.

Costs are not just accounting numbers.They are signals that guide strategic behavior. To understand markets, you must understand how firms think.

Production: Transforming Inputs Into Output

At its core, production is the transformation of inputs into outputs.

Inputs may include:

- Labor
- Capital
- Raw materials
- Technology
- Management expertise
- Information

Outputs are the goods and services sold to consumers.

The relationship between inputs and outputs is captured in what economists call the production function.

The production function reflects how much output can be produced from a given combination of inputs.

But not all inputs adjust at the same speed.

Short Run vs Long Run

The short run is defined by constraint. In the short run, at least one input is fixed.

A factory cannot instantly double in size. A restaurant cannot instantly expand its dining room. A tech company cannot immediately rebuild its infrastructure.

Because some inputs are fixed, adding more of another input eventually leads to diminishing returns.

The long run is defined by flexibility. In the long run, all inputs are variable. Firms can build new facilities. They can adopt new technologies. They can relocate operations. They can restructure production entirely.

Understanding this distinction prevents strategic confusion.

Short run adjustments are tactical. Long run adjustments are structural.

Marginal Product and Diminishing Returns

Marginal Product measures the additional output generated by adding one more unit of an input while holding others constant.

Initially, adding labor may increase output rapidly.

But eventually, diminishing marginal returns set in.

Adding more workers to a fixed space leads to congestion.Machines become overutilized.Coordination becomes inefficient. Diminishing returns is not failure. It is physical reality.

This principle explains why firms cannot expand output indefinitely without expanding capacity.

The Nature of Costs

Costs are the monetary reflection of resource allocation. But economic cost is broader than accounting cost.

There are two major categories:

- Explicit costs: These are direct payments, wages, rent, materials, utilities.
- Implicit costs: These represent opportunity costs, the income foregone by choosing one activity over another.

A business owner who invests personal capital in a company gives up potential investment returns elsewhere. That forgone return is an implicit cost.

Accounting profit ignores implicit costs. Economic profit includes them. This distinction matters.

A firm may appear profitable on paper but generate zero economic profit if opportunity costs are considered.

Long term sustainability depends on economic profit, not accounting profit.

Fixed and Variable Costs

In the short run, firms face two major cost categories:

- Fixed costs: These do not change with output. Rent, insurance, salaries of permanent staff.
- Variable costs: These change with output. Raw materials, hourly labor, shipping costs.

Total cost equals fixed plus variable cost. But decision making depends on marginal cost.

Marginal Cost and Profit Maximization

Marginal Cost is the cost of producing one additional unit of output. Profit maximization occurs where:

Marginal Revenue equals Marginal Cost.

If producing one more unit adds more revenue than cost, production should increase.

If the additional cost exceeds revenue, production should decrease.

This rule appears mechanical, but it is strategic. It determines output level, pricing decisions, and expansion timing.

Economies and Diseconomies of Scale

As firms expand, average costs may fall.

This is called economies of scale.

Large scale production may reduce per unit costs through:

- Bulk purchasing
- Specialized labor
- Technological investment

- Spreading fixed costs

But expansion has limits.

Beyond a certain point, diseconomies of scale emerge.

Management complexity increases. Coordination weakens. Bureaucracy slows decision making. Quality control declines. Bigger is not always better. The goal is optimal scale, not maximum size.

Shutdown Decisions and Loss Minimization

In the short run, firms may continue operating even when unprofitable.

If revenue covers variable costs but not fixed costs, it may still be rational to produce.

If revenue fails to cover variable costs, shutting down minimizes losses.

This decision reflects constraint.In the long run, firms that cannot cover total costs exit the market.

Market entry and exit drive industry adjustment.This is how supply curves form at the industry level.

Production Decisions and Strategic Behavior

Firms do not operate in isolation. Production decisions influence competitors. Overexpansion can lead to oversupply. Oversupply reduces price. Reduced price compresses margins.

In industries with thin margins, strategic production discipline becomes critical.

Firms must anticipate competitor reactions, cost shifts, and demand volatility.Production is not just operational.It is strategic positioning.

Opportunity Cost and Capital Allocation

Perhaps the most important concept in firm behavior is opportunity cost. Capital is scarce. Every dollar invested in one project cannot be invested elsewhere.

Expanding a product line may delay investment in research. Entering a new market may limit domestic growth. Hiring new employees may reduce investment in automation.

Capital allocation determines long term competitive advantage. Microeconomics forces firms to quantify trade offs.

Market Adjustment and Industry Dynamics

In competitive markets:

Economic profit attracts entry.Losses trigger exit. As new firms enter, supply increases. Prices fall. Economic profit disappears.

As firms exit, supply contracts. Prices rise. Remaining firms stabilize. This process tends toward normal profit in competitive industries.

But barriers to entry, regulation, and scale advantages can interrupt this adjustment.

Market structure shapes long term profitability.

Why This Matters for Entrepreneurs and Students

For business owners, production and cost analysis determines survival.

Misjudging marginal cost destroys pricing strategy. Ignoring implicit costs creates illusionary profit. Overexpansion triggers diseconomies. Underinvestment cedes market share.

For students, this chapter reveals how theory translates into firm behavior. Every supply curve is built from cost structures. Every pricing decision reflects marginal analysis. Every industry outcome reflects entry and exit dynamics.

Last Thoughts

Production and cost analysis is not about spreadsheets. It is about disciplined thinking under constraint. Firms exist to transform resources into value.

But resources are scarce. Capital is limited. Time is finite. Information is imperfect.

Economic reasoning does not eliminate uncertainty. It structures it. Understanding production and costs allows you to anticipate adjustment rather than react to it.

Firms that ignore cost signals eventually fail. Firms that understand them can scale strategically. Microeconomics is not about theory for its own sake.

It is about how decisions made inside firms shape the structure of markets.

And markets, in turn, shape opportunity.

Chapter 5: Market Structures, Competition, and Strategic Positioning

Not all markets operate the same way.

Some industries are filled with small competitors fighting for thin margins. Others are dominated by a handful of powerful firms. In some cases, one firm controls nearly the entire market.

Market structure determines pricing power, profitability, innovation, and long term sustainability.

If production explains how firms operate internally, market structure explains how firms behave externally.

To understand competition, you must understand structure.

Why Market Structure Matters

Market structure influences:

- The degree of pricing power firms possess
- The level of competition
- The ease of entry and exit
- The pace of innovation
- The stability of profits
- The role of regulation

Structure shapes behavior.

A firm operating in perfect competition behaves differently than one operating as a monopolist.

Understanding the environment prevents strategic miscalculation.

Perfect Competition

Perfect competition represents a market with:

- Many buyers and sellers
- Identical products
- No single firm able to influence price
- Free entry and exit
- Perfect information

In this structure, firms are price takers.

They accept the market price and adjust output accordingly.

Because products are identical, differentiation is nearly impossible.

Profit margins are thin.Efficiency becomes survival. In the long run, economic profit tends toward zero due to entry and exit.

Perfect competition is rare in pure form but serves as a benchmark.

It demonstrates how decentralized markets allocate resources efficiently when information flows freely and barriers are minimal.

Monopoly

A monopoly exists when a single firm dominates the market and produces a unique product with no close substitutes.

Characteristics include:

- Significant barriers to entry
- Control over price
- Potential for sustained economic profit

Monopolies may arise from:

- Government protection
- Patents
- Control over scarce resources
- Network effects
- Economies of scale

Unlike competitive firms, monopolists are price makers.

They choose output level and price based on demand elasticity and profit maximization.

But monopoly power attracts scrutiny.

Regulation, public backlash, and potential entrants create pressure.

Monopoly is not inherently inefficient, but it concentrates power.

And concentrated power reshapes incentives.

Monopolistic Competition

Monopolistic competition represents a hybrid structure:

- Many firms

- Differentiated products
- Moderate barriers to entry

Products are similar but not identical.

Branding, design, quality, and marketing create perceived differences.

Firms possess limited pricing power because consumers perceive uniqueness.

However, entry remains relatively easy.

In the long run, economic profit tends to decline as new entrants imitate differentiation.

This structure dominates many modern industries:

- Restaurants.
- Clothing brands.
- Technology devices.
- Consumer goods.

Here, competitive advantage depends on differentiation rather than cost alone.

Oligopoly

An oligopoly exists when a small number of large firms dominate the market.

Characteristics include:

- Interdependence
- High barriers to entry
- Strategic behavior
- Potential for collusion

Each firm must consider how rivals will respond to its actions.

Pricing decisions are not independent. Advertising campaigns are not isolated. Innovation races intensify competition.

In oligopolistic markets, firms may:

- Engage in price wars
- Form tacit understandings
- Compete through branding and loyalty
- Invest heavily in research and development

Strategic anticipation becomes central.

Oligopolies often generate stable but tense equilibria.

Monopsony and Oligopsony

While monopoly focuses on sellers, monopsony focuses on buyers.

A monopsony occurs when a single buyer dominates the market.

This structure gives the buyer pricing power over suppliers.

An oligopsony involves a few dominant buyers.

These structures often affect:

- Labor markets
- Agricultural markets
- Specialized manufacturing sectors

Pricing power can exist on either side of the transaction. Power depends on scarcity and alternatives.

Natural Monopoly

A natural monopoly arises when one firm can supply the entire market at lower cost than multiple firms due to high infrastructure costs.

Utilities often fall into this category. In these cases, competition may be inefficient. Regulation attempts to balance efficiency with fairness.

Natural monopolies highlight the tension between scale efficiency and competitive freedom.

Contestable Markets

A market may appear concentrated but remain competitive if entry barriers are low.

The threat of entry disciplines incumbents.

Even a dominant firm may behave competitively if new entrants can easily challenge it.

Barriers to entry determine sustainability of market power.

Barriers to Entry

Market power persists when barriers exist.

Common barriers include:

- High capital requirements
- Regulatory hurdles

- Brand loyalty
- Network effects
- Patents
- Control of distribution channels
- Access to data

Barriers are often subtle.

Sometimes they are legal. Sometimes they are structural. Sometimes they are psychological.

Understanding barriers reveals where opportunity exists.

Market Failure and Government Intervention

Market structures influence efficiency.

Monopoly may lead to:

- Higher prices
- Lower output
- Deadweight loss

But government intervention can also create distortions.

Regulatory capture. Subsidy misallocation. Barriers disguised as protection.

Microeconomics does not assume markets are perfect. Nor does it assume governments are flawless.

Both operate under incentives.

Understanding structure means understanding incentive alignment.

Strategic Positioning Within Structure

For business owners and entrepreneurs:

If operating in perfect competition, focus on cost control. If operating in monopolistic competition, focus on differentiation. If operating in oligopoly, anticipate competitor response. If facing monopoly power, identify niche entry points. If barriers are high, evaluate capital allocation carefully.

Structure determines viable strategy.

Ignoring structure leads to misalignment.

Last Thoughts

Market structure is not academic classification.

It is a map of power.

It reveals who controls pricing. Who influences supply. Who absorbs risk. Who benefits from regulation. Who faces competitive pressure.

Markets are not uniform.

They are ecosystems shaped by incentives, entry conditions, and strategic behavior.

If you understand structure, you understand constraints. If you understand constraints, you understand opportunity.

Microeconomics is not simply about curves and formulas.

It is about how structure shapes behavior, and how behavior shapes outcome.

Chapter 6: Game Theory, Strategic Interaction, and Competitive Behavior

In competitive markets, outcomes do not depend on your decisions alone.

They depend on what others do.

If you lower prices, will competitors follow? If you invest heavily in advertising, will rivals escalate? If you enter a new market, will incumbents fight back?

Game theory studies strategic decision making where each participant's outcome depends on the actions of others.

It forces firms to think beyond immediate profit and consider reaction.

In modern markets, especially concentrated ones, strategic anticipation often determines survival.

What Is a Strategic Game

A strategic game includes:

- Players
- Strategies
- Payoffs

Players can be firms, consumers, governments, or even divisions within a company.

Strategies are the actions available to each player.

Payoffs are the outcomes resulting from combinations of strategies.

The central insight is simple:

Your best move depends on what you expect others to do.

And their best move depends on what they expect you to do.

This interdependence creates complexity.

The Prisoner's Dilemma and Competitive Pressure

One of the most famous examples in game theory is the Prisoner's Dilemma.

It demonstrates how rational self interested behavior can produce outcomes that are worse for everyone involved.

Imagine two competing firms deciding whether to cut prices.

- If neither cuts prices, both earn high profits.
- If one cuts and the other does not, the one who cuts gains market share.
- If both cut prices, profits decline for both.

The rational fear of being undercut may push both firms to cut prices.

The result is lower profit for everyone.

This logic explains:

- Price wars
- Advertising escalation
- Overproduction
- Aggressive competitive tactics

Game theory reveals that individually rational decisions can create collectively inferior outcomes.

Nash Equilibrium

A Nash Equilibrium occurs when each player's strategy is the best response to the other player's strategy.

At this point, no player has an incentive to change strategy unilaterally.

Importantly:

Nash equilibrium does not mean optimal.
It means stable.

In competitive markets, many outcomes represent Nash equilibria.

Firms settle into patterns of behavior because deviation would worsen their position.

Understanding equilibrium allows firms to predict stability points in competition.

Payoff Matrices and Strategic Visualization

A payoff matrix organizes potential outcomes in a grid.

It shows:

- What happens if you choose Strategy A and competitor chooses Strategy B.
- What happens under every combination.

While simplified, payoff matrices force clarity.

They highlight:

- Best case scenarios
- Worst case scenarios
- Dominant strategies
- Vulnerable moves

However, real world strategy rarely has perfect information.

- Payoffs are estimates.
- Competitor intentions are uncertain.
- External shocks alter outcomes.

Game theory is a thinking tool, not a prediction machine.

This is what an empty payoff matrix would look like:

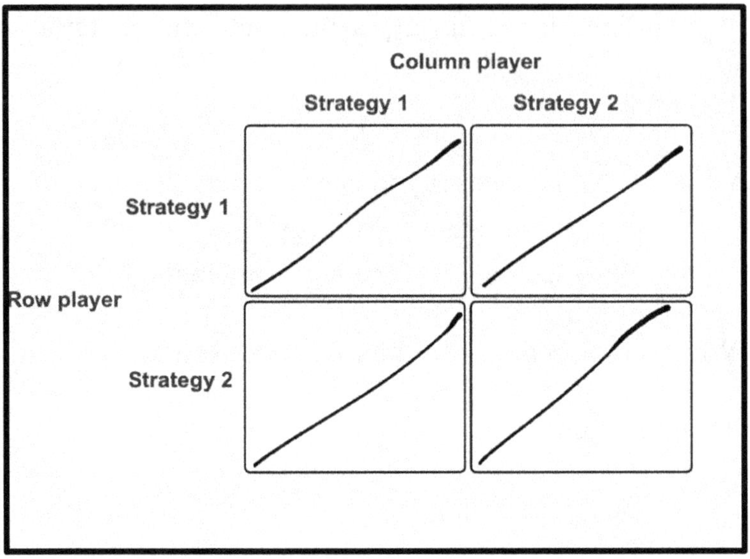

The payoff matrix illustrates potential outcomes across decisions (Fibery, 2024, Figure 3).

Repeated Games and Reputation

Many industries involve repeated interaction.

Firms compete over years, not days.

In repeated games:

Reputation matters. Trust may emerge. Retaliation becomes credible.

A firm that always retaliates against price cuts may deter future aggression.

A firm that never responds invites exploitation.

Strategies such as tit for tat, cooperate initially then mirror opponent behavior, can stabilize competition.

Long term interaction changes incentives.

Credible Threats and Entry Deterrence

Game theory also explains entry deterrence.

An incumbent firm may signal willingness to fight aggressively against new entrants.

This might include:

- Temporarily lowering prices
- Increasing capacity
- Locking in long term contracts
- Investing heavily in advertising

If the threat is credible, potential entrants may stay away.

If the threat lacks credibility, entry occurs.

Credibility depends on cost structure and long term incentive alignment.

Bluffing rarely works in economics.

First Mover and Second Mover Advantage

Timing matters.

In some markets, first movers capture brand loyalty, network effects, or scale advantages.

In others, second movers benefit by learning from mistakes and avoiding early costs.

Game theory analyzes timing as a strategic dimension.

The sequence of moves can change equilibrium outcomes.

Game Theory in Pricing and Advertising

In oligopolistic industries, pricing is strategic.

Aggressive price cuts may increase short term market share but reduce industry profitability.

Advertising spending may escalate if rivals match expenditures.

Firms must evaluate:

- Short term gain
- Long term retaliation
- Industry stability
- Regulatory risk

Strategic restraint may sometimes generate higher long term payoff than aggressive expansion.

Behavioral and Information Limits

Game theory assumes rational players with awareness of strategies.

But real markets include:

- Incomplete information
- Miscalculation
- Overconfidence
- Delayed reaction
- Misinterpreted signals

Firms may misjudge competitor intentions. Competitors may act irrationally. Regulators may intervene unpredictably.

Strategic models simplify reality.They clarify structure but cannot eliminate uncertainty.

Why Game Theory Matters for Entrepreneurs and Students

For business owners:

Game theory encourages forward thinking.

Before making a decision, ask:

How will competitors respond? Is retaliation credible?
Is cooperation possible? What is the long term equilibrium?

For students:

Game theory reveals that markets are not mechanical systems. They are interactive systems.

Outcomes depend on expectation, anticipation, and adaptation.

Last Thoughts

Markets are not just driven by supply and demand.

They are shaped by strategy.

In competitive environments, your move changes the environment itself.

Lowering price changes expectations. Launching a product changes incentives. Investing in capacity changes entry barriers.

Game theory teaches humility.

It reminds us that actions provoke reactions. It shows that equilibrium may not be optimal. It reveals that cooperation and competition coexist.

Microeconomics is not just about individuals and firms responding to prices.

It is about players responding to each other. And in that interaction, markets evolve.

Chapter 7: Market Failure, Externalities, and the Limits of Decentralized Systems

Markets coordinate billions of decisions without central direction.

Prices transmit information. Incentives guide behavior.
Voluntary exchange creates value.

Under certain conditions, markets allocate resources efficiently.

But those conditions are not always present.

When markets fail to allocate resources efficiently, we call it market failure.

Market failure does not mean markets collapse.It means the outcome is not socially optimal.

Understanding these failures allows entrepreneurs, policymakers, and students to see where intervention may be justified and where it may create further distortion.

What Is Market Failure

Market failure occurs when:

- Resources are misallocated
- Social costs exceed private costs
- Social benefits exceed private benefits
- Voluntary exchange fails to produce efficient outcomes

The root causes often include:

- Externalities
- Public goods
- Market power
- Information asymmetry

Markets rely on price signals.When prices fail to capture full cost or benefit, misalignment occurs.

Externalities: When Third Parties Are Affected

An externality exists when a transaction affects a third party who is not directly involved in the exchange.

Externalities can be positive or negative.

Negative Externalities

Negative externalities occur when private actions impose external costs.

Examples include:

- Pollution
- Noise
- Traffic congestion
- Overfishing

If a factory emits pollution, the factory considers its private cost of production.

But nearby residents bear health and environmental costs not reflected in the product's price.

The result:

The market produces too much relative to the socially optimal level.

Price understates true cost.This creates deadweight loss.

Positive Externalities

Positive externalities occur when private actions generate external benefits.

Examples include:

- Education
- Vaccination
- Research and development
- Home maintenance improving neighborhood value

If individuals invest in education, they benefit personally.

But society also benefits from higher productivity and innovation.

Because individuals may not capture full social benefit, markets underproduce these goods relative to the socially optimal level.

Price understates true benefit.

Internalizing Externalities

To correct externalities, policymakers attempt to internalize them.

Common tools include:

- Taxes on negative externalities (Pigouvian taxes)
- Subsidies for positive externalities
- Regulation
- Tradable permits

A carbon tax attempts to align private cost with social cost.A subsidy for education attempts to align private benefit with social benefit.

But intervention introduces its own complexity.

Taxes may overshoot. Subsidies may be misallocated. Regulation may stifle innovation. The key is alignment, not perfection.

Public Goods and Free Rider Problems

Public goods have two defining characteristics:

- Non-excludability, people cannot easily be prevented from using them.

- Non-rivalry, one person's use does not reduce availability to others.

Examples include:

- National defense
- Clean air
- Street lighting
- Basic infrastructure

Because individuals cannot be excluded easily, they may choose not to pay while still benefiting.

This creates the free rider problem.

If everyone waits for others to pay, the good may be underprovided or not provided at all.

Markets struggle to provide public goods efficiently.Government provision often emerges as a solution.

But public provision must still be funded and managed. Efficiency is not guaranteed.

Common Resources and Overuse

Common resources are rival but non-excludable.

Examples include:

- Fisheries
- Public grazing land
- Shared water supplies

These resources are vulnerable to overuse.

If individuals act in self interest without coordination, the resource may be depleted.

This dynamic is sometimes referred to as the tragedy of the commons.

The problem is not greed. It is incentive misalignment. When individuals do not bear the full cost of depletion, overconsumption occurs.

Market Power as Failure

Monopoly and excessive concentration can also generate inefficiency.

When firms restrict output to raise price, society loses mutually beneficial trades.

Deadweight loss emerges again. However, some degree of market power may be necessary to incentivize innovation.

This creates tension between competition and investment incentive.

There is rarely a clean solution.

Government Failure

It is tempting to assume government intervention always improves outcomes.

But policymakers also respond to incentives.

Government failure can arise from:

- Regulatory capture
- Political pressure
- Information gaps
- Bureaucratic inefficiency
- Short term electoral incentives

A poorly designed policy may create larger distortions than the market failure it attempts to solve.

Economic reasoning applies to governments as well.

Strategic Implications for Business

For entrepreneurs and firms:

Understanding externalities can reveal opportunity.

Green innovation can capitalize on negative externality correction.

Education platforms can leverage positive spillover demand. Public private partnerships can fill public good gaps.

Regulatory risk must also be factored into strategic planning. Industries with strong externalities often face regulatory scrutiny. Anticipating policy shifts can become a competitive advantage.

Social Welfare and Trade Offs

Efficiency is not the same as equity.

A market outcome may be efficient but unequal. An intervention may improve equity but reduce efficiency.

Policy decisions often involve balancing:

- Efficiency
- Fairness
- Incentives
- Administrative cost
- Long term innovation

Microeconomics does not provide moral answers.

It provides structural clarity.

Last Thoughts

Markets are powerful coordination systems.

But power does not imply perfection.

When prices fail to reflect full cost or benefit, distortions emerge. When exclusion is impossible, underprovision occurs. When property rights are unclear, overuse follows.

Market failure is not an argument against markets. It is an argument for understanding incentive alignment.

Intervention can correct misalignment. It can also create new distortions.

The real question is not whether markets fail. It is whether alternative systems improve upon them.

Microeconomics trains you to ask that question with discipline rather than emotion.

And in complex systems, discipline matters.

Chapter 8: Information Asymmetry, Moral Hazard, and Incentive Problems

Markets rely on information.

Prices communicate scarcity.Brands signal quality.
Contracts outline expectations.

But what happens when one party knows more than the other?

Information asymmetry occurs when one participant in a transaction has more or better information than the other.

This imbalance can alter behavior, distort markets, and undermine efficiency.

Understanding these dynamics is essential in modern economies where complexity, specialization, and data concentration shape outcomes.

Adverse Selection: When Quality Hides

Adverse selection occurs before a transaction takes place.

It arises when one side of the market cannot accurately distinguish between high quality and low quality offerings.

The classic example is the used car market.

If buyers cannot differentiate between good cars and defective cars, they may only be willing to pay an average price.

High quality sellers exit the market because the price is too low.

Low quality sellers remain.

The market deteriorates.

This phenomenon is sometimes described as the "market for lemons."

Adverse selection reduces overall quality and shrinks mutually beneficial exchange.

It can occur in:

- Insurance markets
- Labor markets
- Financial markets
- Online marketplaces

When information gaps widen, trust erodes.

Moral Hazard: When Behavior Changes After Agreement

Moral hazard occurs after a transaction or contract is established.

It arises when one party takes greater risks because another party bears the cost.

For example:

If a person is fully insured against loss, they may take less precaution.

If banks expect government bailouts, they may engage in excessive risk.

If employees are monitored poorly, effort may decline.

Moral hazard is not about morality. It is about incentive distortion.

When individuals are shielded from consequences, behavior shifts.

Principal Agent Problem

The principal agent problem emerges when one party (the principal) hires another (the agent) to act on their behalf, but their incentives are not perfectly aligned.

Examples include:

- Shareholders and corporate executives
- Voters and elected officials
- Employers and employees
- Clients and financial advisors

If agents pursue personal benefit rather than principal interest, inefficiency results.

Monitoring reduces this problem but increases cost.

Incentive design becomes critical.

Performance based compensation, equity ownership, and contractual alignment attempt to reduce divergence.

Signaling and Screening

Markets adapt to information problems.

Two important mechanisms emerge:

- Signaling: When informed parties take actions to reveal quality. Education credentials signal competence. Brand reputation signals reliability. Warranties signal product durability.
- Screening: When less informed parties design mechanisms to extract information. Insurance companies use questionnaires. Employers conduct interviews. Banks assess credit history.

Signaling and screening attempt to close information gaps.

But they are costly. And imperfect.

Information and Market Efficiency

Perfect competition assumes perfect information.

Reality is far more complex.

Information can be:

- Expensive to acquire
- Strategically withheld
- Manipulated
- Misinterpreted

In financial markets, asymmetric information can lead to:

- Asset bubbles
- Mispricing
- Volatility
- Collapse

In labor markets, asymmetric information can result in wage compression or misallocation of talent.

Information is not neutral. It is strategic capital.

Data, Technology, and Power

In modern economies, data concentration creates new asymmetries.

Large technology firms possess:

- Behavioral data
- Algorithmic insight
- Market analytics

Smaller competitors may lack access to equivalent information.

Information asymmetry becomes structural rather than incidental.

This reshapes competition. Data becomes barrier to entry. Algorithms become strategic assets.

The traditional assumption of equal information becomes increasingly unrealistic.

Regulation and Information Disclosure

Governments often intervene to reduce asymmetry.

Common tools include:

- Disclosure requirements
- Consumer protection laws
- Financial reporting standards
- Licensing requirements

The goal is transparency.

But regulation also introduces cost.

Excessive disclosure may overwhelm rather than clarify. Compliance burdens may deter entry. Regulators themselves may lack complete information.

As always, intervention carries trade offs.

Incentive Design and Institutional Structure

The solution to information asymmetry is not always elimination.

Sometimes it is alignment.

Well designed institutions:

- Align risk and reward
- Clarify accountability
- Reward transparency
- Penalize misrepresentation

Contracts, reputation systems, audits, and performance metrics attempt to create incentive alignment.

Microeconomics teaches that structure influences behavior.

If incentives align, information problems diminish.

If incentives diverge, distortion expands.

Strategic Implications for Entrepreneurs

For business owners and marketers:

Trust is capital.

Reducing customer uncertainty increases demand. Clear communication reduces perceived risk. Reputation lowers screening cost.

For investors:

Information advantage can create opportunity. But overconfidence can create loss.

For policymakers:

Balancing transparency and innovation remains complex. Information shapes power. And power shapes structure.

Last Thoughts

Markets function best when information flows freely.

But information is rarely symmetric. Gaps create risk. Risk alters behavior. Behavior reshapes outcome.

Adverse selection drives quality down. Moral hazard increases risk taking. Principal agent problems distort incentives.

These are not rare anomalies. They are recurring features of real markets. Microeconomics is not the study of idealized systems.

It is the study of constrained, imperfect, incentive driven systems. When information aligns with incentives, coordination improves. When information diverges from incentives, distortion spreads.

Understanding this dynamic allows you to see beneath surface outcomes.

And in modern economies, seeing clearly is often the greatest advantage of all.

Conclusion

Microeconomics begins with small units of analysis.

A consumer choosing between two products. A firm deciding how much to produce. A competitor reacting to a price cut. An investor weighing risk and return.

But when millions of these small decisions occur simultaneously, they create something much larger.

They create markets.

Throughout this book, we examined how:

- Supply and demand coordinate exchange
- Elasticity reveals responsiveness and pricing power
- Utility explains how individuals allocate scarce income
- Production and costs guide firm behavior
- Market structures shape competitive pressure
- Game theory clarifies strategic interaction
- Externalities expose limits of decentralized coordination

- Information asymmetry distorts incentives and outcomes

Each concept stands alone.

But together, they form a framework.

Microeconomics is not just about curves or formulas.

It is about incentives under constraint. Consumers face budget limits. Firms face cost limits. Governments face information limits. Everyone faces trade offs.

Every decision reallocates resources. Every reallocation alters opportunity. Every opportunity carries cost.

When incentives align with accurate information, markets tend to coordinate activity efficiently.

When incentives misalign, distortions emerge.

The power of microeconomics lies in its discipline.

It forces us to ask:

- Who bears the cost?
- Who captures the benefit?

- What alternatives are being sacrificed?
- How will others respond?

It resists simplistic answers.

It acknowledges that:

Markets can generate innovation and efficiency. Markets can also generate inequality and external harm. Government can correct distortions. Government can also introduce new ones. Information empowers decision making. Information asymmetry undermines trust.

Microeconomics does not promise perfection.

It provides clarity.

It trains you to analyze decisions not emotionally, but structurally.

When you understand incentives, you begin to see patterns.

You see why firms hesitate to lower prices. You see why monopolies defend barriers to entry. You see why subsidies alter behavior. You see why insurance changes risk taking. You see why reputation matters. You see why trust is valuable.

Most importantly, you see that outcomes are rarely random.

They are shaped by incentives interacting within constraints.

If macroeconomics studies the economy from above, microeconomics studies it from within.

Macro examines inflation, growth, unemployment, and policy. Micro examines the individual decisions that produce those aggregates.

Together, they form a complete picture.

Small choices create large patterns. Individual incentives create systemic outcomes. Understanding microeconomics gives you more than academic knowledge.

It gives you strategic awareness.

Whether you are a student, entrepreneur, policymaker, or investor, you operate within systems shaped by incentives.

The more clearly you see those incentives, the more deliberately you can act within them.

Microeconomics is not about memorizing models.

It is about disciplined thinking.

And disciplined thinking, in complex systems, is a competitive advantage.

About the Author

Roggie “Raj” Clark is an entrepreneur, author, and education minded creator whose work spans digital marketing, investing, economics, programming, and early academic development. With more than a decade of experience in ecommerce and digital business growth, he has built and managed successful online stores with thousands of sales and consulted for numerous marketing clients on branding, consumer behavior, and online strategy.

As a former marketing manager at a fintech company, Roggie gained firsthand experience in financial systems, wealth building strategy, and economic decision making. That experience inspired him to write books focused on investing, financial literacy, macro and microeconomics, and helping readers make informed long term financial decisions.

Roggie also holds a degree in Elementary Education and has a background in classroom teaching. Drawing from his academic training and educational experience, he has written classroom aligned books designed to support learning standards and structured skill development. His educational titles are intentionally crafted to blend clear instruction with engaging content that supports both classroom and homeschool learning environments.

Whether explaining search engine optimization, programming concepts such as HTML, CSS, and JavaScript, economic principles, or foundational academic skills, Roggie focuses on breaking complex topics into accessible learning experiences. Across every subject he writes about, his goal is to build strong foundations, encourage critical thinking, and equip readers with tools that support long term growth.

He lives in Maryland and continues to develop educational and business focused resources designed to inform, empower, and inspire.

www.ingramcontent.com/pod-product-compliance
Lightning Source LLC
LaVergne TN
LVHW022117200926
848481LV00003B/1180
9798295668692